# Projecting Other Public Inventories for the 2005 RPA Timber Assessment Update

XIAOPING ZHOU, JOHN R. MILLS, AND RICHARD W. HAYNES

A Technical Document Supporting
the USDA Forest Service Interim Update of the 2000 RPA Assessment

U.S. DEPARTMENT OF AGRICULTURE    FOREST SERVICE

## Authors

**Xiaoping Zhou** is a forester, **John R. Mills** and **Richard W. Haynes** are research foresters, Forestry Sciences Laboratory, P.O. Box 3890, Portland, OR 97208.

# Abstract

**Zhou, Xiaoping; Mills, John R.; Haynes, Richard W. 2007.** Projecting other public inventories for the 2005 RPA timber assessment update. Gen. Tech. Rep. PNW-GTR-717. Portland, OR: U.S. Department of Agriculture, Forest Service, Pacific Northwest Research Station. 31 p.

This study gives an overview of the current inventory status and the projection of future forest inventories on other public timberland. Other public lands are lands administered by state, local, and federal government but excluding National Forest System lands. These projections were used as part of the 2005 USDA Forest Service Resource Planning Act timber assessment update. The projections were made by region and forest type by using the modified Aggregated Timberland Assessment System and the forest inventory data with methods and procedures consistent with the methods used for private and national forest inventory projections. Although the projected inventory volume differs by region, both softwood and hardwood inventories on other public timberlands in the United States are projected to increase over 60 percent during the next 50 years. Forest net growth exceeds harvest in most regions pushing inventory volumes up. The one exception is the Pacific Northwest East (ponderosa pine region) where the softwood inventory is expected to decrease until 2030 owing to lower softwood net growth and then slowly increase. The mature and old mature stands for both softwood and hardwood are projected to increase significantly for all regions especially in the South region where proportion of mature and old mature increases from 9 to 54 percent for softwood and 4 to 55 percent for hardwood.

Keywords: Other public timberlands, timber supply, modeling, inventory projection, yield function, forest structure, public policy, seral stage.

# Introduction

The past two decades have seen significant efforts in developing consistent ways of describing and projecting timber inventories by region and owner. Among other purposes, these projections are used in the timber assessments required by the Forest and Rangeland Renewable Resource Planning Act (RPA) of 1974. Summaries for harvest, growth, and inventories are key parts of an RPA timber assessment (see tables 16 and 17 in Haynes 2003). These summary tables and their predecessors have shaped public perceptions of both the magnitudes and trends in total U.S. forest inventories and resource conditions. They also illustrate the relative contributions of different owners and regions. The states making up the various regions are shown in table 1. The traditionally recognized ownerships for forest resource information include national forest, other public, forest industry, and nonindustrial private forest owners. Here we focus on the other public ownership, which includes the U.S. Department of the Interior's National Park Service, Bureau of Land Management, and Fish and Wildlife Service; U.S. Department of Defense and U.S. Department of Energy; other federal, state, and local (county, municipal, etc.), and nonfederal public.

One of the goals of the assessment process has been to develop consistent inventory projection approaches for all timberland owners across all regions so that all resource conditions (regardless of owner) could be summarized comparably. This started following the 1980 assessment (USDA FS 1982), when efforts focused on increasing the amount of detail represented in the forest inventory projection models. The first step was the implementation of the Aggregate Timberland Assessment System (ATLAS; Mills and Kincaid 1992) for private timberland owners in the 1990 RPA timber assessment (Haynes 1990). At that time, the ability to produce detailed projections for public owners was limited because the inventory system used by U.S. Department of Agriculture, Forest Service Forest Inventory and Analysis (FIA) was not applied to national forest lands in the West. During the 1990s, the scope of FIA data broadened to include consistent data for all ownerships. The 2000 RPA timber assessment (Haynes 2003) included the implementation of expanded forest management intensities on private lands and the first detailed set of inventory projections made for the national forest lands. Here we describe the completion of this process with the inclusion of the other public ownership into the inventory projection system. This ownership has about 10 percent of the timberland in the United States, that is, about 50.3 million acres (table 2) including Alaska. These projections were developed for the 2005 RPA timber

**One of the goals of the assessment process has been to develop consistent inventory projection approaches for all timberland owners across all regions so that all resource conditions (regardless of owner) could be summarized comparably.**

**Table 1—Other public forest Forest and Rangeland Renewable Resource Planning Act (RPA) regions**

| RPA region | Region name | States |
|---|---|---|
| 0 | Pacific Northwest West | Western Oregon, western Washington |
| 1 | Pacific Northwest East | Eastern Oregon, eastern Washington |
| 2 | Pacific Southwest | California |
| 3 | Rocky Mountain North | Idaho, Montana |
| 4 | Rocky Mountain South | Arizona, Colorado, Nevada, New Mexico, South Dakota, Utah, Wyoming |
| 5 | North Central, Plains States | Illinois, Indiana, Iowa, Kansas, Missouri, Nebraska, Ohio |
| 6 | North Central, Lake States | Michigan, Minnesota, Wisconsin, North Dakota |
| 7 | Northeast | Connecticut, Delaware, Maine, Maryland, Massachusetts, New Hampshire, New Jersey, New York, Pennsylvania, Rhode Island, Vermont, West Virginia |
| 8 | South Central | Alabama, Arkansas, Kentucky, Louisiana, Mississippi, Oklahoma, Tennessee, Texas |
| 9 | Southeast | Florida, Georgia, North Carolina, South Carolina, Virginia |
| 10 | Alaska | Alaska (not projected with the model) |

**Table 2—Status of other public forest land by region**

| Region | Total forest land | Timberland | Other forest land |
|---|---|---|---|
| | *Thousand acres* | | |
| Pacific Northwest West | 6,283 | 4,594 | 1,689 |
| Pacific Northwest East | 2,340 | 1,000 | 1,340 |
| Pacific Southwest | 4,964 | 383 | 4,581 |
| Rocky Mountain North | 4,753 | 3,152 | 1,601 |
| Rocky Mountain South | 27,616 | 2,964 | 24,652 |
| Plains States | 2,847 | 1,960 | 887 |
| Lake States | 14,623 | 13,020 | 1,603 |
| Northeast | 12,754 | 7,921 | 4,833 |
| South Central | 6,060 | 5,082 | 978 |
| Southeast | 7,340 | 4,899 | 2,441 |
| Alaska | 80,539 | 5,321 | 75,218 |
| Total area | 170,119 | 50,296 | 119,823 |

assessment update (Haynes and others 2007), and will provide, for the first time since the 1980 assessment, a consistent inventory projection across all ownerships.

For the past two decades, inventory projections for other public ownerships were made by using a growth-drain identity[1] and assumed harvest and growth levels extrapolated from historical trends. The latest projections using the growth-drain identity were done for the 2000 RPA timber assessment and are shown in figure 1. These projections suggest that softwood and hardwood inventories would follow similar trajectories and increase in the future. In terms of the total contribution to the national inventory, the other public ownership averages about 17 percent of the U.S. inventory volume over the 100-year period. Changing definitions and inventory designs of the other public ownership, especially the 1991 transfer of American Indian or tribal timberlands from the other public to the nonindustrial private ownership group, complicates making general observations about past trends in resource conditions.

The purpose of this paper is twofold. First, we describe the input information and assumptions necessary to use the same techniques and assumptions for the other public ownership as were used for other ownership groups. This involves the modification of the ATLAS inventory projection system and structuring the data sets in management units around timber types and described by age class. Second, we present a set of inventory projections for the other public ownership for use in national inventory summaries, and we discuss the contributions of the other public landowners to broad-scale concerns associated with forest structure.

**In terms of the total contribution to the national inventory, the other public ownership averages about 17 percent of the U.S. inventory volume over the 100-year period.**

## Current Status of Other Public Timberland

The most recent periodic inventory data for each state were assembled from the 2002 RPA database (Smith and others 2004), and it is used as a starting point of the inventory projections. There are 749 million acres of forest land in the United States, of which about 20 percent is included in national forests, 23 percent is in other public ownership, and the remainder is privately owned. A subset of 504 million acres is considered timberland. By definition, timberland is forest land that is capable of producing at least 20 cubic feet per acre per year of industrial wood in natural stands, and not withdrawn from timber utilization or administrative regulation. Across the four ownership categories there are large differences in the proportion of forest land that is classified as timberland. For example, 83 percent of all

---

[1] The growth-drain identity is expressed as $I_t = I_{t-1} + G - H$ where $I_t$ is inventory in period $t$, $G$ is the periodic net growth, and $H$ is the periodic removals between periods $t$ and $t$-1.

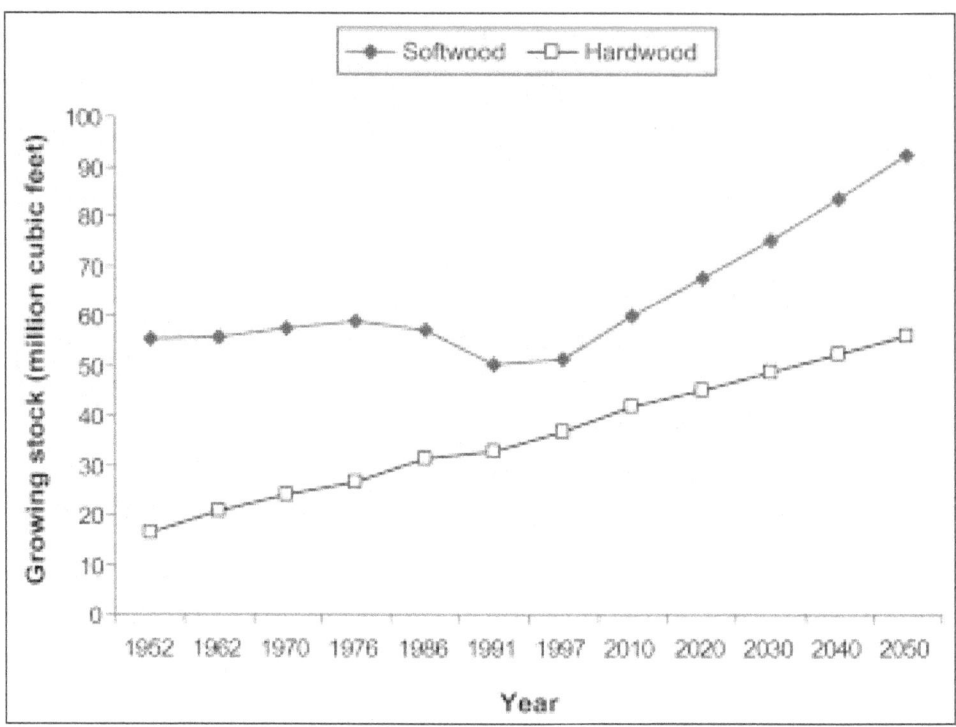

Figure 1—Other public inventory projected by using the growth-drain formulation. (Source: Haynes 2003).

privately owned forest land is timberland, 65 percent of the national forests forest land is timberland, but only 30 percent of the other public forest land is timberland (50 percent if excluding Alaska). This implies that on average, forest lands in other public ownership are less productive than forest lands in the other ownerships. This also reflects that other public ownership has a greater portion of forest land in the reserved category than any other ownership. In fact, the forest lands owned by National Park Service and Departments of Defense and Energy are almost all reserved. Other public timberland distribution differs across regions.[2] The current areas of other public forest land by region based on the 2002 RPA database are shown in table 2. For the 48 continental states, most of the other public forest land is located in the Rocky Mountain, North Central (Plains States plus the Lake States), and Northeast regions. Although the Rocky Mountain South region has the largest number of forest-land acres outside of Alaska, only 11 percent is timberland. A similar situation exists for the Pacific Southwest and the

---

[2] The RPA timber assessment divides the 48 continental states into 10 assessment regions.

Pacific Northwest East regions, where less than half of the forest land is classified as timberland. Alaska, with about 7 percent of forest land in timberland, is unique, but Alaska and Hawaii are not included in the ATLAS projections.

Figure 2 also helps to reveal a difference in public timberland land ownership patterns between the Eastern and Western United States. The map in figure 2 was derived from FIA plot data and shows the approximate plot locations where other public timberland was encountered (based on fuzzed and swapped plot coordinates[3]). It shows that the other public ownership is more broadly distributed in the East where it is often in relatively small parcels interspaced among other timberland owners. Figure 2 also illustrates that there are relatively few places with large blocks of contiguous other public timberlands. National forests are typically in larger parcels, and most of the publicly owned timberland in the East is in other public ownership, whereas most of the publicly owned timberland in the West is in national forests. The following tabulation (in millions of acres, not including Alaska) shows that Western national forests dominate the public timberland arena:

| Area | National forests | Other public |
|------|------------------|--------------|
| East | 21.1 | 32.9 |
| West | 71.1 | 12.1 |

**Most of the publicly owned timberland in the East is in other public ownership, whereas most of the publicly owned timberland in the West is in national forests.**

Figure 3 shows the initial distribution of other public timberland area by stand age and broad region based on the 2002 RPA database. The North has about 50 percent of the other public timberland, and consequently those forests dominate the appearance of the forest inventory structure. Inventories in the South are significantly younger than those in the North and West. Ninety-five percent of other public timberland in the South is less than 50 years old, whereas this is true for only 38 percent of the northern and 32 percent of the western timberland. Within the North, 86 percent of stands are less than 100 years old and about 9 percent are older than 150 years; whereas in the West, about 76 percent of other public timberland is less than 100 years old and 9 percent is equal to or older than 150 years. Compared with other regions, the West shows a more uniform age distribution.

---

[3] By law, any data tied to an individual landowner in nonpublic land cannot be disclosed. So the plot location in the database is moved (plus/minus) up to a mile (fuzzed), and up to 5 percent of private plots may have their locations switched with similar plots (swapped).

Figure 2—Other public timberland distribution.

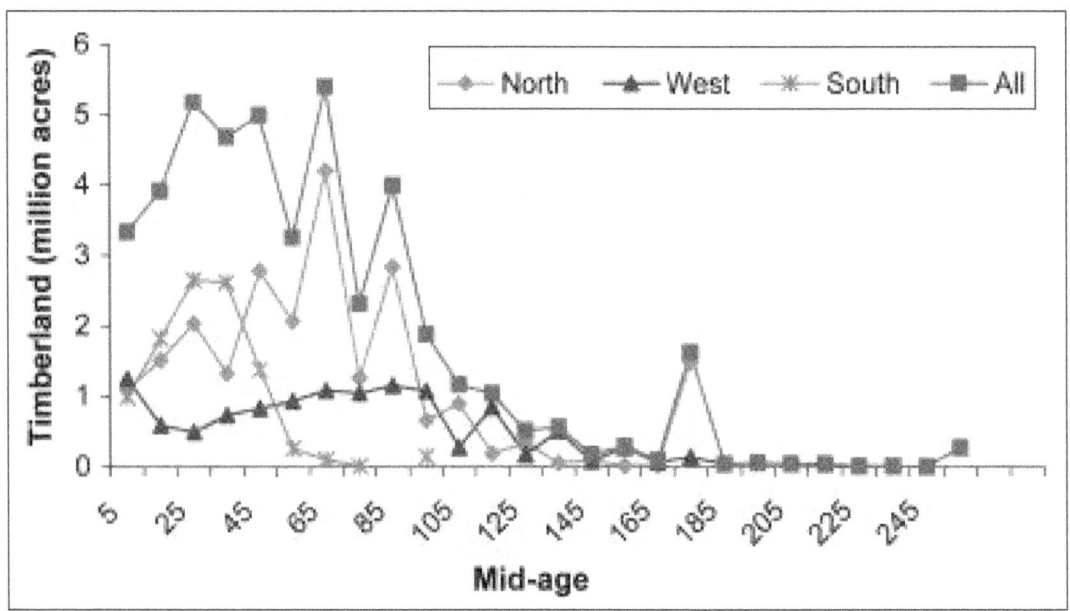

Figure 3—Initial distributions (2002) of other public timberland area by region and age. Note: The bump of areas at age class 175 represents an aggregation of all stands in the North of 175 and older.

# Projection Model and Assumptions

The inventory projections for other public ownerships are modeled by using the same methods as those used for the private (both forest industry and nonindustrial private forests) and national forest ownerships. This involves using an updated version of ATLAS (Mills and Kincaid 1992). The inventory was structured in ATLAS much the same way it was structured to project national forest inventories (Mills and Zhou 2003). Basic assumptions involve the inventory stratification, the development of yield functions for each forest type and region, assumptions about mortality, the development of management intensity classes, the assumption concerning harvest levels and harvest methods, as well as any area change assumptions. The following section will provide some detail regarding these assumptions.

**Age classes—**

Timberland in the East was stratified into 18 age classes. Because the western public lands generally support some of the oldest forests, the West was stratified into 26 age classes in an effort to better identify potential late-seral-stage conditions. A 10-year stand age interval for age class was used for all regions except the South where the inventory was aggregated into 5-year classes. In the periodic FIA inventory, stand age is the average total age, to the nearest year, of the trees in the predominant stand-size class of the condition (determined using local procedures). The various seral stage[4] definitions are the same here as used in other RPA applications (Haynes 2003). The intent of using these classes is to help quantify forest development and to provide a sense of forest structure.

**Yield functions—**

Yield tables for other public timberland were developed for each forest type in a region by using the FIA plot and tree information. These procedures were also applied to national forest (Mills and Zhou 2003). Each plot record contains empirical growth rates that embody the effects of historical and recent management

---

[4] Seral stage—A stage or recognizable condition of a plant community that occurs during its development from bare ground to climax. Used here, forests are assumed to progress through five recognized stages: seedlings (age 5 all regions and fiber except North softwood, which includes 5 to 15); poles and saplings (age 25 to 35 North softwood; 15 to 35 North hardwood; 10 to 15 South softwood; 10 to 20 South hardwood; 15 to 35 West hardwood and softwood); young (age 45 to 65 North; 20 to 35 South softwood; 25 to 55 South hardwood; 45 to 75 West softwood; 45 to 55 West hardwood); mature (age 75 to 135 North; 40 to 75 South softwood; 60 to 75 South hardwood; 85 to 135 West softwood; 65 to 135 West hardwood); and old mature (age 145+ North; 80+ South; 145+ West). These stages are represented by grouping age classes. The age-class groupings differ by broad regions reflecting successional differences among various timber types.

practices. The simple statistical regression against the age class was used to estimate the net annual growth, and the yields were then an accumulation of net annual growth. The following tabulation represents the approach to develop a yield table for a 10-year-interval age classification:

| Age class | Net growth | Yield |
|-----------|-----------|-------|
| 0 | $G_0$ | $Y_0 = 0$ |
| 1 | $G_1$ | $Y_1 = (G_0 + G_1)/2 \times 5$ |
| 2 | $G_2$ | $Y_2 = (G_1 + G_2)/2 \times 10 + Y_1$ |
| 3 | $G_3$ | $Y_3 = (G_2 + G_3)/2 \times 10 + Y_2$ |
| 4 | $G_4$ | $Y_4 = (G_3 + G_4)/2 \times 10 + Y_3$ |
| ... | ... | ... |

Where $G_{ac}$ = net growth ($ft^3 \cdot yr^{-1} \cdot acre^{-1}$) at age class $ac$.

$Y_{ac}$ = yield at age class $ac$.

The variable $Y_{ac}$ represents the net growing-stock volume ($ft^3$/acre) at the age class midpoint (e.g., for ac = 0, age = 5; for ac = 1, age = 15; and when ac = 2, age = 25, etc.). The general model of the net growth ($G$) as a function of age class ($ac$) is expressed as $G = f(ac)$. This can be illustrated for the Douglas-fir forest type on other public timberland in the Pacific Northwest West region (for age classes greater than zero (ac>0)) as:

$$G_{ac} = 506.8 - 33.06ac + 0.96\,ac^2 - 143.96e^{(1/ac)} \qquad (ac>0) \qquad (1)$$

Values from the solution of equation (1) for the first eight age classes for Douglas-fir are shown in the following tabulation:

| Age range | Age class | Growth $_{age\ class}$ |
|-----------|-----------|------------------------|
| *Years* | | *Cubic feet per acre* |
| 0 to 10 | 0 | |
| 10 to 20 | 1 | 83.4 |
| 21 to 30 | 2 | 207.2 |
| 31 to 40 | 3 | 215.3 |
| 41 to 50 | 4 | 205.1 |
| 51 to 60 | 5 | 189.7 |
| 61 to 70 | 6 | 172.9 |
| 71 to 80 | 7 | 156.4 |
| ... | ... | ... |

In regions with very few observations from other public timberlands, yields were constructed by adding FIA plots from private lands. In the South, the yield functions for national forest were used for other public timberlands assuming that forests in both ownerships would have similar yield trajectories. For the Pacific Northwest West, because of their small proportion, pines were grouped with the fir and spruce timber type. The complete set of yield tables developed for each region can be found in appendix tables 6 to 14.

There is a critical assumption in the use of these empirical yield functions; assuming the future conditions will be similar to those in the recent past. If future conditions differ significantly from those in the past, then this approach is subject to bias. For example, management practices, atmospheric pollution, climate change, and use of improved genotypes can influence future growth compounding errors associated with using empirical data to project stands forward (Adlard 1995).

**Mortality—**

As canopy closure occurs in a stand with differential tree growth, the slower growing trees become suppressed leaving them less resistant to the effects of weather (drought and wind), insects, and disease (Oliver and Larson 1990). So as forest stands age and average tree diameter increases, the number of living trees in the stand typically decreases owing to mortality of trees unable to compete for the limited resources (Davis and Johnson 1987). Oliver and Larson (1990) identified two categories of mortality, regular mortality and irregular mortality. On a landscape scale, regular mortality is part of forest succession, occurring as trees age and compete with each other for light and water. Meanwhile, irregular mortality is associated with disturbances such as fire, insect epidemics, or disease that kill what are otherwise healthy trees. Mortality is measured by successive surveys and counted as the volume in the trees that have died over a fixed interval.

The starting forest inventory data were compiled by FIA to represent net values for all volumes (growth, inventory, removals), and consequently the projections represent net values as well. Net values consider only live trees. Net annual growth is the average annual net increase in the volume of trees during the period between inventories (Smith and others 2004). Using net values to calibrate the growth models is an implicit approach to considering mortality. For example, the growth-and-yield relationships were developed from a cross section of field plots, many of which represent stands that would be expected to have past histories with various levels of mortality. For a handful of plots, net growth was reported to be a negative value, meaning the volume of mortality exceeded the gross increment from growth.

This likely indicates a recent disturbance to the stand. These plots were included in the process to calibrate net inventory growth, so this background level of mortality is part of the projection. On a landscape level, we assert these projections reflect the average rate of historical mortality.

**Management intensity—**
Other public timberland projections allow three management regimes that differ by the approach to harvest. The first allows regeneration harvest, that is, a final harvest or clearcut will occur in these stands at a range of ages typically followed by the planting of seedlings. The second regime was developed to apply a partial harvest—this treatment removes a portion of volume to mimic a stand subject to multiple entries. The third management option is labeled no-harvest, as these stands are projected forward in time but not subjected to harvesting. Acres are enrolled into these management intensities upon regeneration; and the amount moving into any one regime depends on the acres of final harvest and the enrollment rates set for that regime. Harvest is set to occur at younger ages in the South than in the West, reflecting the rate stands mature into various product classes. The number of acres treated for harvest in a regime depends on the harvest request and relative available volume within the regime.

**Area change—**
The area of other public timberland is assumed to remain unchanged for the next 50 years. The model is flexible for implementing area and forest type changes, but for public lands these transitions are occurring more slowly than on private lands where urbanization, agriculture, changing land ownership, and management objectives play a dynamic role in shaping timberlands.

**Site class—**
Other public timberland covers a range of site productivity from 20 to more than 225 cubic feet of net growth per acre per year as measured at the culmination of mean annual increment. Most other public timberland in the Pacific Northwest West produces, for example, over 120 cubic feet per acre per year, whereas other regions generally produce less. Because there were insufficient data to tailor the other public management regimes for different site classes, yield functions representing an average site class were used in making projections.

**Harvest projections—**
Harvest for the other public owners is assumed to be set by various agency policies. In 1997, removals from other public ownerships were 948 million cubic feet. We

extrapolated projections of future harvest for this owner from past trends. These projected harvests generally increase reflecting the observed propensity of many agencies to increase harvest as inventory and net growth increases. This tendency follows sustained yield management practices. Given the diversity of land management agencies, other assumptions would be difficult to develop. Several of the state land management agencies are obligated to manage for high returns to support school common (trust) funds.

**Other parameters—**

Several other parameters are required for an ATLAS projection. These contribute to the calibration of growth, the assignment of stocking upon regeneration, the proportion of hardwood and softwood fiber in the inventory, and the descriptive variables such as average diameter by age. These empirical values are derived from variables from the FIA plot and tree data (see Mills 1990, Mills and Kincaid 1992 for their relevance).

**Assumptions for forest land excluded from harvest—**

Although presented in the area summary tables (table 2), projections include only timberland. That is, they do not include forest land officially reserved (wilderness areas, national parks, etc.) or lands classified as nonproductive forest land. Across the broader landscape, these latter areas are important contributors to ecosystem diversity, provide wildlife habitat, sequester carbon dioxide from the atmosphere, and provide other ecosystem services, such as clean water and recreational opportunities. Data are not yet available to project these forests but may become available in the future as the need for various broad-scale studies evolves.

## Projection Results

The removals from other public timberland are projected to increase for both softwoods and hardwoods for the next five decades as shown in tables 3 and 4. Softwood removals are projected to increase by 25 percent from 553 million to 691 million cubic feet by 2050, whereas hardwood removals will increase by 20 percent from 381 million to 456 million cubic feet. The relative change in the projected level of removals is expected to differ significantly by region, however. Softwood removals decline in the Northeast, Pacific Southwest, and Pacific Northwest East by 29, 52, and 45 percent, respectively. Whereas the North Central is relatively stable, large increases occur in the Southeast (14 percent), South Central (24 percent), Rocky Mountains (184 percent), and Pacific Northwest West (39 percent). Alaska was not projected with ATLAS but rather a growth-drain table was

**The removals from other public timberland are projected to increase for both softwoods and hardwoods for the next five decades.**

**Table 3—Softwood inventory, annual removals, and net annual growth projected for other public timberland**

| Region | 1997 | 2002 | Projections | | | | |
|---|---|---|---|---|---|---|---|
| | | | 2010 | 2020 | 2030 | 2040 | 2050 |
| | | | *Million cubic feet* | | | | |
| Northeast: | | | | | | | |
| Removals | 13 | 14 | 12 | 12 | 11 | 10 | 10 |
| Inventory | 2,797 | 3,111 | 3,414 | 3,798 | 4,185 | 4,564 | 4,923 |
| Net annual growth | 61 | 63 | 47 | 50 | 49 | 47 | 45 |
| North Central: | | | | | | | |
| Removals | 71 | 59 | 59 | 57 | 57 | 56 | 56 |
| Inventory | 5,272 | 5,275 | 6,320 | 7,415 | 8,488 | 9,560 | 10,586 |
| Net annual growth | 141 | 141 | 164 | 165 | 164 | 161 | 158 |
| Southeast: | | | | | | | |
| Removals | 114 | 112 | 101 | 108 | 115 | 123 | 128 |
| Inventory | 4,452 | 4,577 | 5,677 | 6,154 | 6,217 | 6,291 | 6,385 |
| Net annual growth | 145 | 155 | 174 | 124 | 127 | 137 | 138 |
| South Central: | | | | | | | |
| Removals | 61 | 63 | 60 | 67 | 70 | 75 | 78 |
| Inventory | 1,951 | 2,179 | 2,210 | 2,431 | 2,517 | 2,550 | 2,579 |
| Net annual growth | 66 | 81 | 92 | 81 | 78 | 80 | 83 |
| Rocky Mountains: | | | | | | | |
| Removals | 49 | 51 | 92 | 112 | 125 | 139 | 145 |
| Inventory | 8,427 | 8,503 | 9,777 | 10,661 | 11,208 | 11,503 | 11,646 |
| Net annual growth | 168 | 169 | 211 | 190 | 174 | 164 | 157 |
| Pacific Southwest:[a] | | | | | | | |
| Removals | 23 | 23 | 9 | 11 | 11 | 11 | 11 |
| Inventory | 1,320 | 1,320 | 1,412 | 1,517 | 1,622 | 1,719 | 1,811 |
| Net annual growth | 29 | 29 | 20 | 22 | 21 | 21 | 20 |
| Pacific Northwest West:[b] | | | | | | | |
| Removals | 159 | 159 | 210 | 222 | 222 | 221 | 221 |
| Inventory | 19,243 | 19,243 | 22,495 | 25,835 | 29,172 | 32,505 | 35,766 |
| Net annual growth | 491 | 459 | 545 | 556 | 550 | 551 | 542 |
| Pacific Northwest East:[b] | | | | | | | |
| Removals | 67 | 67 | 49 | 48 | 44 | 40 | 37 |
| Inventory | 2,537 | 2,539 | 2,458 | 2,401 | 2,371 | 2,392 | 2,449 |
| Net annual growth | 67 | 27 | 42 | 42 | 42 | 42 | 43 |

**Table 3—Softwood inventory, annual removals, and net annual growth projected for other public timberland (continued)**

| | | | Projections | | | | |
|---|---|---|---|---|---|---|---|
| Region | 1997 | 2002 | 2010 | 2020 | 2030 | 2040 | 2050 |
| | | | *Million cubic feet* | | | | |
| Alaska: | | | | | | | |
| Removals | 5 | 5 | 5 | 5 | 5 | 5 | 5 |
| Inventory | 5,090 | 5,090 | 5,637 | 6,129 | 6,621 | 7,112 | 7,604 |
| Net annual growth | 40 | 54 | 54 | 54 | 54 | 54 | 54 |
| United States: | | | | | | | |
| Removals | 562 | 553 | 597 | 642 | 660 | 680 | 691 |
| Inventory | 51,089 | 51,837 | 59,400 | 66,341 | 72,401 | 78,196 | 83,749 |
| Net annual growth | 1,208 | 1,178 | 1,349 | 1,284 | 1,259 | 1,257 | 1,240 |

Note: In 1991, Native American lands were transferred to nonindustrial private forest; previously they were in other public.

Note: Historical harvest data are estimates of harvest trends and differ somewhat from the estimates of actual consumption shown in some tables. For the projection years, the data show the average volume that would be harvested given the assumptions of the study.

[a] Pacific Southwest excludes Hawaii.

[b] Pacific Northwest West (western Oregon and western Washington) is also called the Douglas-fir subregion, and Pacific Northwest East (eastern Oregon and eastern Washington) is also called the ponderosa pine subregion.

Source: Haynes and others 2007.

**Table 4—Hardwood inventory, annual removals, and net annual growth projected for other public timberland**

| | | | Projections | | | | |
|---|---|---|---|---|---|---|---|
| Region | 1997 | 2002 | 2010 | 2020 | 2030 | 2040 | 2050 |
| | | | *Million cubic feet* | | | | |
| Northeast: | | | | | | | |
| Removals | 45 | 51 | 50 | 54 | 54 | 55 | 55 |
| Inventory | 10,158 | 11,018 | 11,838 | 12,747 | 13,761 | 14,735 | 15,693 |
| Net annual growth | 151 | 194 | 138 | 150 | 154 | 151 | 150 |
| North Central: | | | | | | | |
| Removals | 231 | 189 | 172 | 180 | 181 | 180 | 179 |
| Inventory | 11,430 | 11,538 | 13,561 | 15,546 | 17,446 | 19,326 | 21,255 |
| Net annual growth | 237 | 305 | 369 | 375 | 369 | 370 | 371 |
| Southeast: | | | | | | | |
| Removals | 39 | 54 | 52 | 58 | 67 | 76 | 81 |
| Inventory | 4,062 | 4,262 | 4,418 | 4,595 | 4,680 | 4,695 | 4,664 |
| Net annual growth | 100 | 106 | 75 | 76 | 77 | 78 | 78 |
| South Central: | | | | | | | |
| Removals | 53 | 51 | 54 | 67 | 79 | 92 | 101 |
| Inventory | 4,956 | 5,728 | 6,095 | 7,110 | 7,909 | 8,499 | 8,859 |
| Net annual growth | 181 | 146 | 165 | 161 | 153 | 141 | 133 |

**Table 4—Hardwood inventory, annual removals, and net annual growth projected for other public timberland (continued)**

| Region | 1997 | 2002 | Projections | | | | |
|---|---|---|---|---|---|---|---|
| | | | 2010 | 2020 | 2030 | 2040 | 2050 |
| | *Million cubic feet* | | | | | | |
| Rocky Mountains: | | | | | | | |
| Removals | 2 | 1 | 3 | 3 | 3 | 3 | 3 |
| Inventory | 823 | 827 | 746 | 866 | 985 | 1,099 | 1,222 |
| Net annual growth | 45 | 18 | 13 | 15 | 15 | 15 | 14 |
| Pacific Southwest:[a] | | | | | | | |
| Removals | 1 | 1 | 1 | 1 | 1 | 1 | 1 |
| Inventory | 319 | 319 | 332 | 384 | 433 | 478 | 512 |
| Net annual growth | 5 | 5 | 4 | 5 | 5 | 4 | 4 |
| Pacific Northwest: | | | | | | | |
| Removals | 13 | 33 | 27 | 29 | 31 | 32 | 34 |
| Inventory | 2,846 | 2,846 | 3,331 | 3,828 | 4,377 | 4,894 | 5,389 |
| Net annual growth | 74 | 64 | 77 | 82 | 85 | 84 | 82 |
| Alaska: | | | | | | | |
| Removals | 1 | 1 | 1 | 1 | 1 | 1 | 1 |
| Inventory | 1,930 | 2,260 | 2,696 | 3,400 | 4,105 | 4,810 | 5,514 |
| Net annual growth | 49 | 72 | 72 | 72 | 72 | 72 | 72 |
| United States: | | | | | | | |
| Removals | 386 | 381 | 361 | 394 | 418 | 441 | 456 |
| Inventory | 36,524 | 38,798 | 43,017 | 48,476 | 53,696 | 58,536 | 63,108 |
| Net annual growth | 841 | 910 | 913 | 936 | 930 | 915 | 904 |

Note: In 1991, Native American lands were transferred to nonindustrial private forest; previously they were in other public.

Note: Historical harvest data are estimates of harvest trends and differ somewhat from the estimates of actual consumption shown in some tables. For the projection years, the data show the average volume that would be harvested given the assumptions of the study.

[a] Pacific Southwest excludes Hawaii.

Source: Haynes and others 2007.

constructed and the results included in table 3. Alaska's softwood removals represent less than 1 percent of the total. It should be noted that although smaller in area than the Northern and Southern regions, the Pacific Northwest West region tops other public softwood production in 2050 with removals that represent 32 percent of the United States total. The combined Rocky Mountain region comes in at second place with 21 percent of the removals in 2050. Meanwhile, when it comes to hardwood production, the East shows its dominance with 91 percent of all other public hardwood removals. Whereas most regions show stable hardwood removals projections, the Southeast and South Central regions show increases of 50 and 98 percent, respectively. This increase in removals is concurrent with increasing demand for hardwoods on private land in the South (Haynes and others 2007).

Most inventories on other public timberlands are expected to rise. Nationally, both softwood and hardwood inventories are projected to increase over 60 percent by 2050. As shown in figure 4, the age class distribution of inventory shifts to the right as stands age faster than they are harvested. Regionally, the projection varies for softwoods, ranging from a 3 percent loss in Pacific Northwest East (ponderosa pine region) to a 100 percent gain in North Central region. The most variation seen for softwoods is in the Pacific Northwest East where inventories are expected to decrease until 2030 and then increase slowly, when the level of removals is expected to be in balance with the amount of growth in that region. Hardwood inventory is projected to increase across all regions, from 9 percent in Southeast to 89 percent in the Pacific Northwest region.

The initial (2002) distribution of inventory by age in the West (fig. 5a) shows two large peaks, one at age 0 to 10 (mid-age 5) and the other at age 80 to 90 (mid-age 85). The relatively large number of acres in the first age class represents both poorly stocked or recently regenerated areas. The drop in area around age 15 and 25 suggests there was a decade of high harvesting, fire mortality, and/or a recent history of poor regeneration. There is a sharp decline in area past age 100, suggesting that harvesting has been concentrated in stands age 100 or greater.

**Nationally, both softwood and hardwood inventories are projected to increase over 60 percent by 2050.**

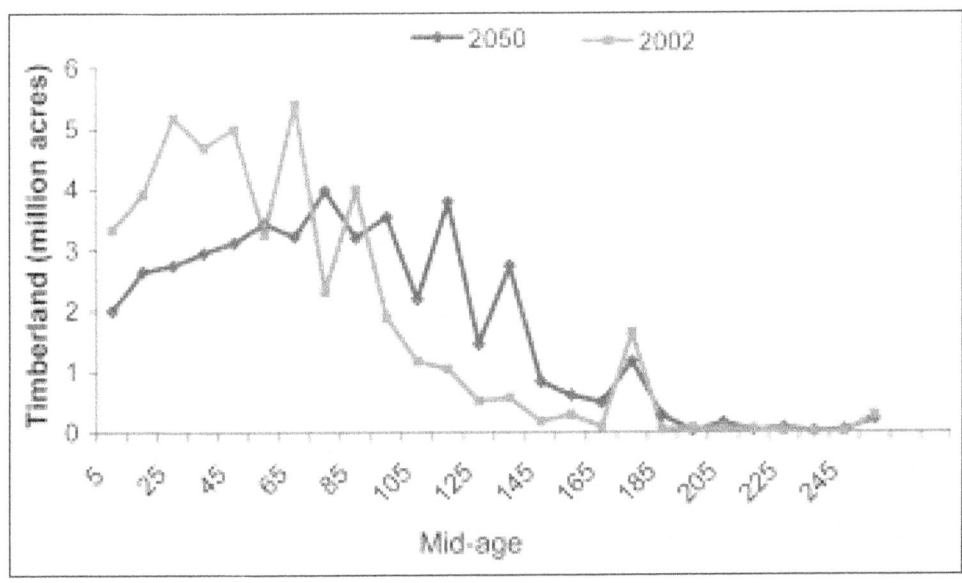

Figure 4—Initial and projected distributions (2050) of other public timberland area by age.
Note: The bump of acres at age class 175 represent an aggregation of all stands in the north of 175 and older

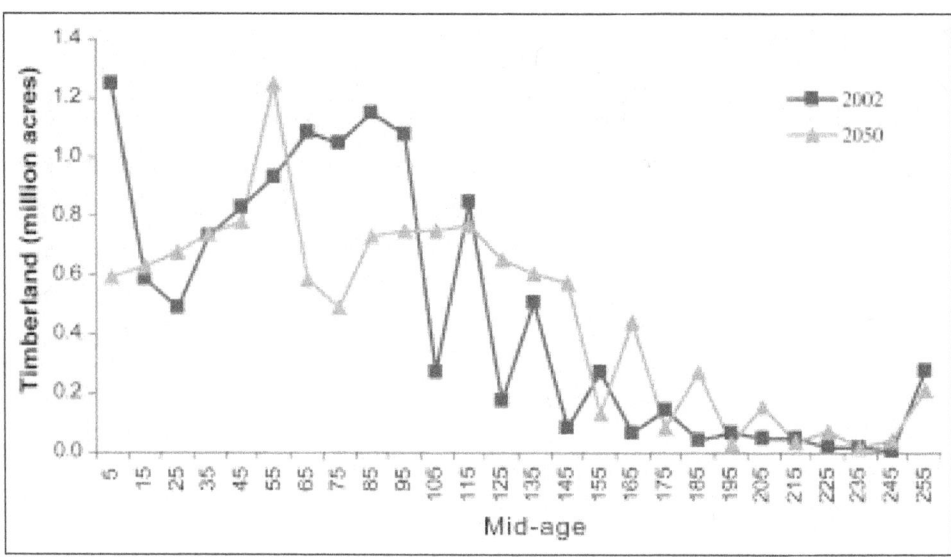

Figure 5a—Initial and projected distribution of other public timberland area in the Western United States.

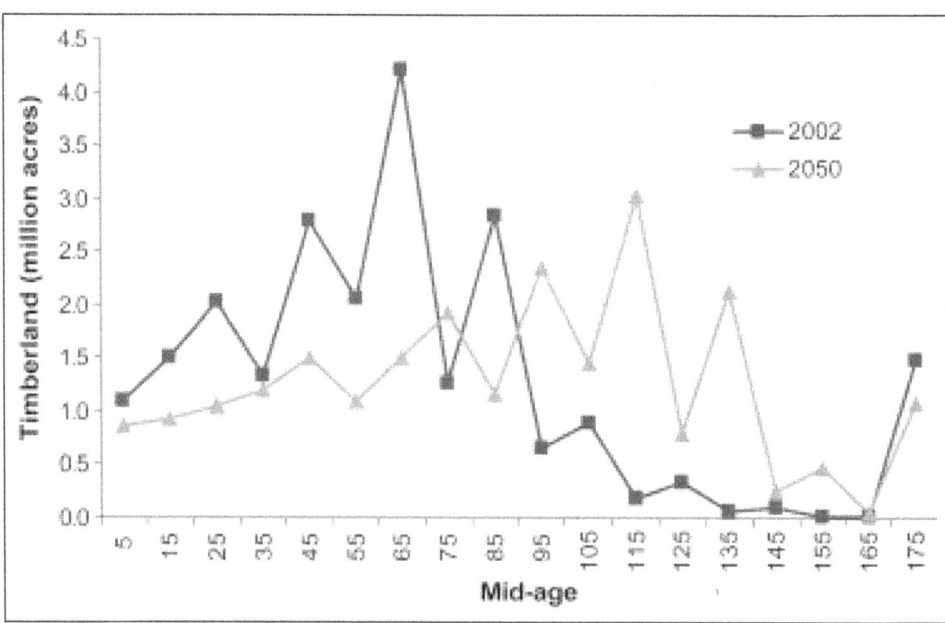

Figure 5b—Initial and projected distribution of other public timberland area in the Northern United States.

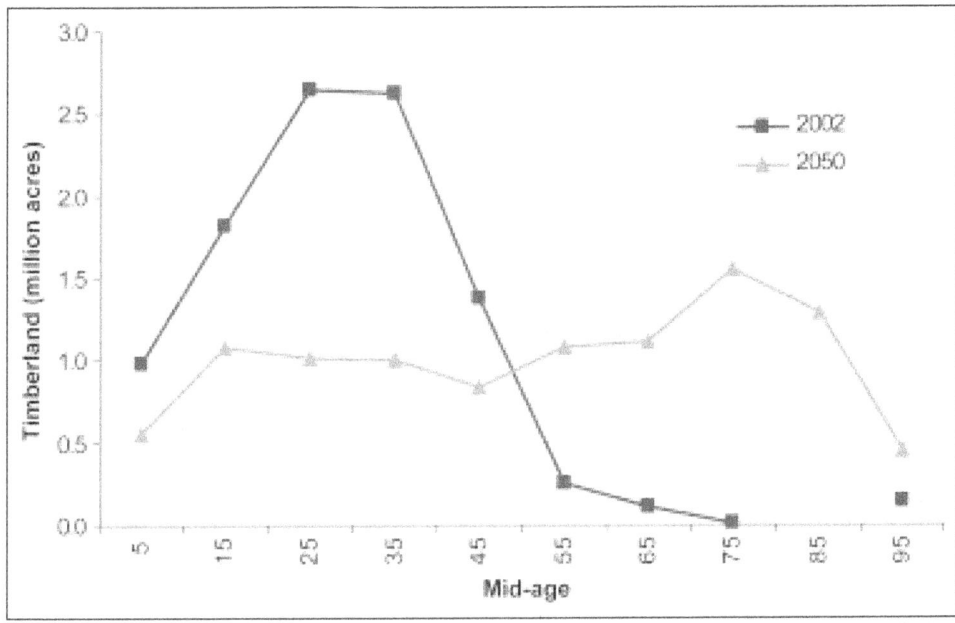

Figure 5c—Initial and projected distribution of other public timberland area in the Southern United States.

During the projection, harvesting occurred over a range of age classes with minimums set around age 85. Under age 60, there are roughly the same number of acres as there were at the start of the projection, but past age 100 there are more as harvest levels have been less than growth.

In 2002, the other public inventory in the North is nearly all less than 110 years old (see fig. 5b). The spike at 175 represents all area supporting stands older than 170, and there are as many acres there as there are between ages 100 and 170. This could indicate a history of harvest by age 100 for most of the ownership while some areas continue to support late-successional stands. The projection moves the 25- to 85-year-old bulge of inventory ahead, harvesting over the range from 40 to 60. The resulting inventory has significantly fewer acres less than age 50, indicating less harvest than in the last 50 years, and the gap between age 100 and 170 has been nearly filled. In all, the projection shows a more balanced representation across nearly all age classes.

Nearly all of the initial Southern other public inventory is less than 60 years old (see fig. 5c). Southern rotations are much shorter than anywhere else, as it can be seen that after age 40 the area decreases dramatically. By 2050 the area less than age 50 declines from 95 to 45 percent, while the area over 50 increases signifi- cantly. This is an indication that harvest in the next 50 years will be less than it has been in recent history. Like the North, the projected inventory shows more balance among a greater range of age classes.

Finally, these results depend on assumptions about management objectives and harvest behaviors of a diverse collection of county, state, and federal agencies who manage the other public timberlands. Each of these agencies differs in purpose, legislative mandates, and relations to stakeholder groups. For example, harvests from Oregon state lands in 2005 were 341 million board feet, but this could change dramatically (say 50 percent) depending on future state forest policies, outcomes from planning processes, or court cases.

Overall, the mid-age classes (stands from age 70 to less than 150) are expected to increase dramatically from 26 percent in 2002 to 48 percent in 2050 (shown in fig. 4), timberland area for stands over 150 is expected to be stable. In 2002, 5.6 percent of the other public timberlands had stands over 150 years. This is only expected to increase to 7 percent by 2050 under the current removal and disturbance assumptions, and most of that increase comes in the Western region, from 8 percent to 12 percent.

## Discussion

Figure 6 shows a comparison between the inventory volume projections on other public timberland from the 2000 RPA timber assessment (Haynes 2003) that used the simple growth-drain identity and the current 2005 RPA timber assessment update, which applies the same inventory projection system to other public timberland as used for private and National Forest System timberlands. In general, improving the rigor of inventory projections for other public ownership does not change much of the essential projection of total inventory volume. That is, they are projected to increase for both hardwood and softwoods. The 2000 RPA timber inventory levels on other public timberland shown in figure 6 are higher for softwoods (9 percent) but lower for hardwoods (12 percent) than the levels in 2005 RPA timber assessment update.

**This 2005 RPA update approach does, however, produce other information that leads to a richer understanding of the resource conditions on other public timberlands.**

This 2005 RPA update approach does, however, produce other information that leads to a richer understanding of the resource conditions on other public timberlands. For example, we can use several indicators from the Montreal Process (Montreal Process Technical Advisory Committee 2000) to describe the overall condition of this ownership. These indicators are inventory volumes by hardwood and softwood, the growth removals ratio, and proportions by seral stages. Examining these gives us a broad-scale understanding of both timber and ecological conditions. In general, these indicators suggest well-managed forests where excess growth leads to higher inventory levels and proportionally older stands (especially those in the mature seral stage).

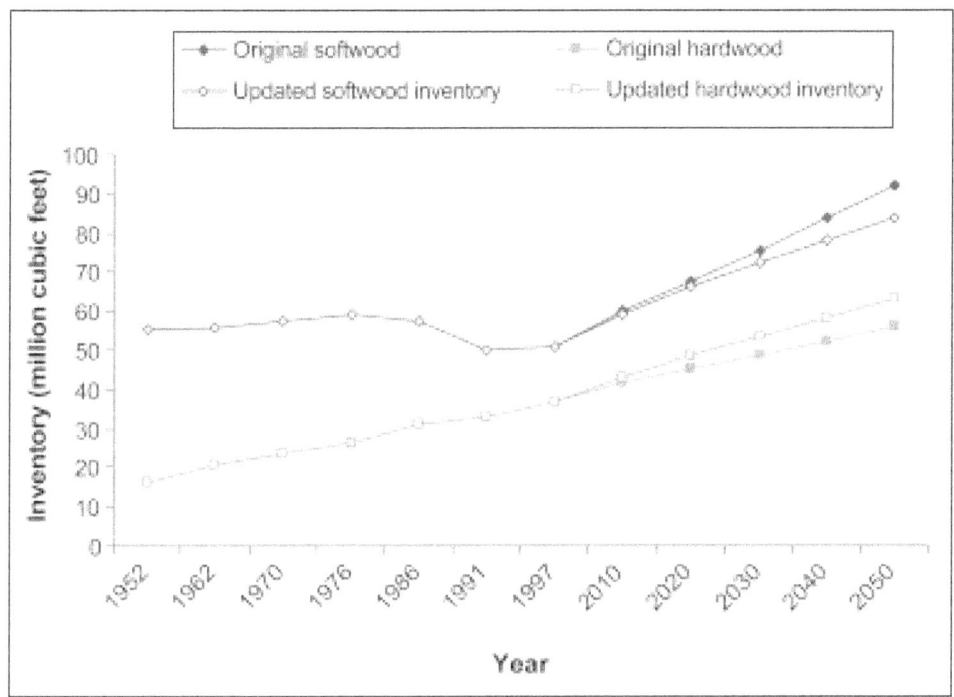

Figure 6—Other public inventory comparing original and updated data.

The structure of this inventory is projected to change over the projection period (table 5). Currently, the other public ownership is about the same as the structure for all private timberlands with the exception of having a higher proportion (15 percent more) young sawtimber stands. Over time, like the other ownerships, other public timberlands tend to age with a reduction in the area of young stands (table 5). The rate of this progression is faster than for private timberlands but substantially less than the progression on national forest timberlands where the area in younger (seedlings, poles-saplings, and young seral stages) stands drops from 42 to 24 percent by 2050. This suggests that a larger proportion of other public timberlands follow some sort of sustained yield or structure-based management approach to forest regulation rather than the ecosystem management approaches now common on national forest timberlands.

The growth and aging of the inventories is due in part to the relatively high growth-to-drain ratios for softwoods and hardwoods. These can be summarized from tables 3 and 4 and shown as follows:

| Species | 2002 | 2050 |
|---|---|---|
| Softwoods | 2.15 | 1.79 |
| Hardwoods | 2.18 | 1.98 |

Table 5–Other public timberlands by seral stages

| Species and area | Seral stage | | | | | |
|---|---|---|---|---|---|---|
| | Seedling[a] | Poles-saplings[b] | Young[c] | Mature[d] | Old mature[e] | Total |
| Softwood: | | | *Thousand acres* | | | |
| North— | | | | | | |
| 2000 | 657 | 1,221 | 2,404 | 1,627 | 362 | 6,270 |
| 2010 | 688 | 1,058 | 2,001 | 2,288 | 235 | 6,270 |
| 2020 | 682 | 657 | 2,099 | 2,605 | 228 | 6,270 |
| 2030 | 514 | 688 | 1,590 | 3,267 | 210 | 6,270 |
| 2040 | 442 | 682 | 1,345 | 3,505 | 296 | 6,270 |
| 2050 | 399 | 514 | 1,058 | 3,925 | 374 | 6,270 |
| South— | | | | | | |
| 2000 | 523 | 1,191 | 2,336 | 381 | 5 | 4,436 |
| 2010 | 293 | 822 | 2,547 | 773 | 1 | 4,436 |
| 2020 | 294 | 578 | 2,013 | 1,544 | 8 | 4,436 |
| 2030 | 277 | 586 | 1,400 | 2,160 | 12 | 4,436 |
| 2040 | 296 | 565 | 1,164 | 2,327 | 84 | 4,436 |
| 2050 | 303 | 597 | 1,151 | 2,107 | 278 | 4,436 |
| West— | | | | | | |
| 2000 | 1,109 | 1,469 | 3,262 | 3,643 | 979 | 10,463 |
| 2010 | 706 | 1,996 | 2,930 | 3,602 | 1,228 | 10,463 |
| 2020 | 677 | 2,335 | 2,426 | 3,870 | 1,156 | 10,463 |
| 2030 | 626 | 2,493 | 2,152 | 3,644 | 1,549 | 10,463 |
| 2040 | 583 | 2,010 | 2,578 | 3,772 | 1,521 | 10,463 |
| 2050 | 550 | 1,885 | 2,703 | 3,451 | 1,874 | 10,463 |
| Hardwood: | | | | | | |
| North— | | | | | | |
| 2000 | 810 | 3,287 | 6,654 | 4,619 | 1,260 | 16,630 |
| 2010 | 1,104 | 3,300 | 4,178 | 6,936 | 1,112 | 16,630 |
| 2020 | 924 | 3,057 | 4,050 | 7,452 | 1,147 | 16,630 |
| 2030 | 817 | 2,838 | 3,287 | 8,577 | 1,112 | 16,630 |
| 2040 | 726 | 2,845 | 3,300 | 8,335 | 1,425 | 16,630 |
| 2050 | 671 | 2,467 | 3,057 | 8,942 | 1,492 | 16,630 |

**Table 5–Other public timberlands by seral stages (continued)**

| Species and area | Seral stage | | | | | |
| --- | --- | --- | --- | --- | --- | --- |
| | Seedling[a] | Poles-saplings[b] | Young[c] | Mature[d] | Old mature[e] | Total |
| Softwood: | *Thousand acres* | | | | | |
| South— | | | | | | |
| 2000 | 463 | 1,156 | 3,691 | 95 | 140 | 5,545 |
| 2010 | 175 | 915 | 4,128 | 210 | 117 | 5,545 |
| 2020 | 201 | 540 | 3,812 | 862 | 129 | 5,545 |
| 2030 | 220 | 620 | 2,576 | 1,947 | 182 | 5,545 |
| 2040 | 242 | 671 | 1,721 | 2,396 | 516 | 5,545 |
| 2050 | 244 | 717 | 1,538 | 1,582 | 1,465 | 5,545 |
| West— | | | | | | |
| 2000 | 142 | 346 | 286 | 744 | 111 | 1,629 |
| 2010 | 74 | 336 | 297 | 807 | 114 | 1,629 |
| 2020 | 63 | 286 | 276 | 886 | 118 | 1,629 |
| 2030 | 55 | 279 | 194 | 971 | 130 | 1,629 |
| 2040 | 48 | 192 | 212 | 1,047 | 131 | 1,629 |
| 2050 | 43 | 165 | 216 | 1,005 | 199 | 1,629 |

[a] Seedlings seral stage = age 5 all regions and fiber except North softwood, which includes 5 to 15.
[b] Poles and saplings seral stage = age 25 to 35 North softwood; 15 to 35 North hardwood; 10 to 15 South softwood; 10 to 20 South hardwood; 15 to 35 West hardwood and softwood.
[c] Young sawtimber seral stage = age 45 to 65 North; 20 to 35 South softwood; 25 to 55 South hardwood; 45 to 75 West softwood; 45 to 55 West hardwood.
[d] Mature sawtimber seral stage = age 75 to 135 North; 40 to 75 South softwood; 60 to 75 South hardwood; 85 to 135 West softwood; 65 to 135 West hardwood.
[e] Old mature sawtimber seral stage = age 145+ North; 80+ South; 145+ West.
Source: Haynes and others 2007.

At present, growth is more than twice harvest levels. But in both cases the ratio is projected to drop because harvest increases at a somewhat faster rate than the rate for growth. Growth rates for both fiber types start to decline (after peaking in 2020) reflecting higher proportions of the inventories moving to slower growing older age classes. In the ATLAS approach, growth rates are expressed by age classes, and net growth drops in older age classes reflecting maturing trees and higher mortality (see app. tables 6-14).

These increases in inventories (from 1,031 to 1,665 cubic feet per acre for softwoods) pose additional management challenges especially in the West where there is a need to manage fuel conditions on public lands. These projections suggest that fuel loading will only increase and, without increased management, pose greater challenges in the future. The volumes involved suggest that fuel management strategies will be complicated by the need for repeated treatments.

**These projections suggest that fuel loading will only increase and, without increased management, pose greater challenges in the future.**

In general, the various indicators of other public inventories suggest a group of well-managed timberlands. Many public land managers are active participants in efforts to demonstrate how the United States is making progress toward sustainable forest management. These are also the public timberlands most frequently encountered by residents in the Eastern United States. In that context, they will play a significant role in shaping perceptions of the links between forest management and the flow of forest goods and services.

## Metric Equivalents

| When you know: | Multiply by: | To find: |
| --- | --- | --- |
| Acres | 0.405 | Hectares |
| Cubic feet | .0283 | Cubic meters |
| Cubic feet per acre | .07 | Cubic meters per hectare |

## Literature Cited

**Adlard, P.G. 1995**. Myth and reality in growth estimation. Forest Ecology and Management. 71(3): 171–176.

**Davis, L.S.; Johnson, K.N. 1987**. Forest management. New York: McGraw-Hill, Inc. 790 p.

**Forest and Rangeland Renewable Resources Planning Act of 1974 [RPA]**; 16 U.S.C. 1601 (note).

**Haynes, R.W., coord. 1990.** An analysis of the timber situation in the United States: 1989–2040. Gen. Tech. Rep. RM-199. Fort Collins, CO: U.S. Department of Agriculture, Forest Service, Rocky Mountain Forest and Range Experiment Station. 286 p.

**Haynes, R.W., tech. coord. 2003**. An analysis of the timber situation in the United States: 1952–2050. Gen. Tech. Rep. PNW-GTR-560. Portland, OR: U.S. Department of Agriculture, Forest Service, Pacific Northwest Research Station. 254 p.

**Haynes, R.W.; Adams, D.M.; Alig, R.J.; Ince, P.J.; Mills, J.R.; Zhou, X. 2007.** The 2005 timber assessment update. Gen. Tech. Rep. PNW-GTR-699. Portland, OR: U.S. Department of Agriculture, Forest Service, Pacific Northwest Research Station. 212 p.

**Mills, J.R. 1990**. Developing ATLAS growth parameters from forest inventory plots. In: LaBau, V.; Cunia, T., eds. State-of-the-art methodology of forest inventory: a symposium proceedings. Gen. Tech. Rep. PNW-GTR-263. Portland, OR: U.S. Department of Agriculture, Forest Service, Pacific Northwest Research Station: 112–118.

**Mills, J.R.; Kincaid, J.C. 1992**. The aggregate timberland assessment system— ATLAS: a comprehensive timber projection model. Gen. Tech. Rep. PNW-GTR-281. Portland, OR: U.S. Department of Agriculture, Forest Service, Pacific Northwest Research Station. 160 p.

**Mills, J.R.; Zhou, X. 2003**. Projecting national forest inventories for the 2000 RPA timber assessment. Gen. Tech. Rep. PNW-GTR-568. Portland, OR: U.S. Department of Agriculture, Forest Service, Pacific Northwest Research Station. 58 p.

**Montreal Process Technical Advisory Committee. 2000.** Technical notes, criteria 1-6. http://www.mpci.org/tac/mexico/tn1-6_e.html. (October 2006).

**Oliver, C.D.; Larson, B.C. 1990**. Forest stand dynamics. New York: McGraw-Hill, Inc. 467 p.

**Smith, B.W.; Miles, P.D.; Vissage, J.S.; Pugh, S.A. 2004**. Forest resources of the United States, 2002. Gen. Tech. Rep. NC-241. St. Paul, MN: U.S. Department of Agriculture, Forest Service, North Central Research Station. 137 p.

**U.S. Department of Agriculture, Forest Service [USDA FS]. 1982.** An analysis of the timber situation in the United States 1952–2030. Forest Resour. Rep. 23. Washington, DC. 272 p. [plus appendicies].

# Appendix

**Table 6—Yield tables for other public Pacific Northwest West region by forest type**

| Age class | Douglas-fir | Western hemlock | Fir and spruce | Red alder | Hardwood mix |
|---|---|---|---|---|---|
| | | | *Cubic feet per acre* | | |
| 5 | 0 | 0 | 0 | 0 | 0 |
| 15 | 208 | 150 | 72 | 267 | 47 |
| 25 | 1,661 | 1,754 | 779 | 1,265 | 657 |
| 35 | 3,774 | 4,470 | 1,926 | 2,866 | 1,724 |
| 45 | 5,876 | 7,262 | 3,057 | 4,530 | 2,798 |
| 55 | 7,849 | 9,938 | 4,093 | 6,166 | 3,798 |
| 65 | 9,662 | 12,440 | 5,013 | 7,748 | 4,704 |
| 75 | 11,309 | 14,750 | 5,812 | 9,273 | 5,510 |
| 85 | 12,794 | 16,866 | 6,497 | 10,747 | 6,222 |
| 95 | 14,128 | 18,794 | 7,074 | 12,180 | 6,847 |
| 105 | 15,325 | 20,548 | 7,554 | 13,583 | 7,394 |
| 115 | 16,399 | 22,139 | 7,947 | 14,971 | 7,874 |
| 125 | 17,367 | 23,584 | 8,266 | 16,323 | 8,298 |
| 135 | 18,245 | 24,900 | 8,523 | 17,613 | 8,678 |
| 145 | 19,052 | 26,104 | 8,731 | 18,843 | 9,026 |
| 155 | 19,805 | 27,214 | 8,903 | 20,013 | 9,354 |
| 165 | 20,523 | 28,250 | 9,051 | 21,123 | 9,676 |
| 175 | 21,223 | 29,229 | 9,191 | 22,173 | 10,004 |
| 185 | 21,924 | 30,171 | 9,334 | 23,163 | 10,351 |
| 195 | 22,645 | 31,095 | 9,494 | 24,093 | 10,729 |
| 205 | 23,405 | 32,021 | 9,685 | 24,963 | 11,152 |
| 215 | 24,222 | 32,968 | 9,921 | 25,773 | 11,634 |
| 225 | 25,114 | 33,955 | 10,215 | 26,523 | 12,186 |
| 235 | 26,102 | 35,003 | 10,581 | 27,213 | 12,822 |
| 245 | 27,204 | 36,132 | 11,032 | 27,843 | 13,555 |
| 255 | 28,438 | 37,360 | 11,583 | 28,413 | 14,399 |

**Table 7—Yield tables for other public Pacific Northwest East region by forest type**

| Age class | Ponderosa pine | Douglas-fir and larch | True fir | Lodgepole pine | Hardwood |
|---|---|---|---|---|---|
| | | *Cubic feet per acre* | | | |
| 5 | 0 | 0 | 0 | 0 | 0 |
| 15 | 21 | 85 | 0 | 95 | 32 |
| 25 | 279 | 581 | 217 | 583 | 261 |
| 35 | 747 | 1,287 | 745 | 1,168 | 585 |
| 45 | 1,257 | 2,055 | 1,392 | 1,722 | 891 |
| 55 | 1,774 | 2,826 | 2,063 | 2,234 | 1,166 |
| 65 | 2,287 | 3,571 | 2,711 | 2,706 | 1,413 |
| 75 | 2,790 | 4,274 | 3,308 | 3,142 | 1,631 |
| 85 | 3,278 | 4,927 | 3,840 | 3,544 | 1,825 |
| 95 | 3,750 | 5,527 | 4,302 | 3,916 | 1,996 |
| 105 | 4,204 | 6,075 | 4,691 | 4,261 | 2,145 |
| 115 | 4,640 | 6,573 | 5,010 | 4,580 | 2,275 |
| 125 | 5,057 | 7,024 | 5,264 | 4,876 | 2,388 |
| 135 | 5,454 | 7,435 | 5,459 | 5,150 | 2,483 |
| 145 | 5,830 | 7,812 | 5,602 | 5,403 | 2,563 |
| 155 | 6,186 | 8,160 | 5,704 | 5,637 | 2,628 |
| 165 | 6,522 | 8,489 | 5,773 | 5,854 | 2,680 |
| 175 | 6,836 | 8,805 | 5,822 | 6,053 | 2,718 |
| 185 | 7,129 | 9,117 | 5,860 | 6,237 | 2,744 |
| 195 | 7,400 | 9,434 | 5,901 | 6,405 | 2,758 |
| 205 | 7,650 | 9,765 | 5,956 | 6,559 | 2,763 |
| 215 | 7,879 | 10,118 | 6,037 | 6,699 | 2,763 |
| 225 | 8,086 | 10,503 | 6,159 | 6,825 | 2,763 |
| 235 | 8,271 | 10,930 | 6,333 | 6,939 | 2,763 |
| 245 | 8,434 | 11,408 | 6,574 | 7,041 | 2,763 |
| 255 | 8,576 | 11,948 | 6,895 | 7,132 | 2,763 |

**Table 8—Yield tables for the Pacific Southwest region by forest type**

| Age class | Pinyon juniper | True fir | Hardwood | Douglas-fir and redwood | Ponderosa pine | Mixed conifer |
|---|---|---|---|---|---|---|
| | | | *Cubic feet per acre* | | | |
| 5 | 0 | 0 | 0 | 0 | 0 | 0 |
| 15 | 0 | 28 | 0 | 58 | 5 | 29 |
| 25 | 11 | 196 | 15 | 397 | 66 | 159 |
| 35 | 26 | 463 | 370 | 832 | 205 | 349 |
| 45 | 47 | 840 | 1,090 | 1,250 | 415 | 636 |
| 55 | 73 | 1,343 | 1,826 | 1,660 | 689 | 1,028 |
| 65 | 103 | 1,954 | 2,493 | 2,076 | 1,024 | 1,523 |
| 75 | 137 | 2,652 | 3,072 | 2,510 | 1,411 | 2,114 |
| 85 | 173 | 3,419 | 3,564 | 2,970 | 1,845 | 2,793 |
| 95 | 211 | 4,239 | 3,979 | 3,461 | 2,321 | 3,548 |
| 105 | 251 | 5,099 | 4,328 | 3,987 | 2,832 | 4,368 |
| 115 | 291 | 5,989 | 4,620 | 4,552 | 3,372 | 5,240 |
| 125 | 332 | 6,899 | 4,868 | 5,156 | 3,935 | 6,152 |
| 135 | 372 | 7,822 | 5,082 | 5,801 | 4,516 | 7,090 |
| 145 | 410 | 8,750 | 5,269 | 6,487 | 5,107 | 8,041 |
| 155 | 447 | 9,678 | 5,440 | 7,214 | 5,703 | 8,990 |
| 165 | 481 | 10,600 | 5,600 | 7,980 | 6,299 | 9,924 |
| 175 | 511 | 11,511 | 5,758 | 8,785 | 6,887 | 10,828 |
| 185 | 537 | 12,408 | 5,919 | 9,627 | 7,463 | 11,687 |
| 195 | 558 | 13,286 | 6,089 | 10,505 | 8,020 | 12,488 |
| 205 | 574 | 14,143 | 6,273 | 11,417 | 8,551 | 13,216 |
| 215 | 584 | 14,974 | 6,478 | 12,360 | 9,052 | 13,856 |
| 225 | 587 | 15,778 | 6,706 | 13,334 | 9,515 | 14,394 |
| 235 | 587 | 16,551 | 6,961 | 14,335 | 9,936 | 14,814 |
| 245 | 587 | 17,291 | 7,249 | 15,361 | 10,307 | 15,102 |
| 255 | 587 | 17,997 | 7,572 | 16,410 | 10,624 | 15,242 |

**Table 9—Yield tables for the Rocky Mountain North region by forest type**

| Age class | Douglas-fir | Ponderosa pine | Fir-spruce | Lodgepole pine | Hardwood | High-elevation softwoods |
|---|---|---|---|---|---|---|
| | | | *Cubic feet per acre* | | | |
| 5 | 0 | 0 | 0 | 0 | 0 | 0 |
| 15 | 30 | 72 | 0 | 63 | 20 | 27 |
| 25 | 266 | 372 | 260 | 365 | 132 | 153 |
| 35 | 665 | 679 | 880 | 762 | 309 | 312 |
| 45 | 1,137 | 977 | 1,626 | 1,239 | 589 | 499 |
| 55 | 1,641 | 1,262 | 2,390 | 1,784 | 960 | 713 |
| 65 | 2,158 | 1,531 | 3,118 | 2,383 | 1,334 | 951 |
| 75 | 2,674 | 1,783 | 3,782 | 3,022 | 1,660 | 1,210 |
| 85 | 3,183 | 2,021 | 4,365 | 3,689 | 1,915 | 1,486 |
| 95 | 3,680 | 2,246 | 4,862 | 4,369 | 2,093 | 1,778 |
| 105 | 4,163 | 2,458 | 5,271 | 5,050 | 2,201 | 2,082 |
| 115 | 4,629 | 2,662 | 5,596 | 5,717 | 2,253 | 2,395 |
| 125 | 5,078 | 2,858 | 5,842 | 6,358 | 2,272 | 2,715 |
| 135 | 5,511 | 3,050 | 6,018 | 6,959 | 2,276 | 3,039 |
| 145 | 5,929 | 3,240 | 6,133 | 7,506 | 2,276 | 3,363 |
| 155 | 6,333 | 3,431 | 6,199 | 7,987 | 2,276 | 3,686 |
| 165 | 6,725 | 3,626 | 6,227 | 8,387 | 2,276 | 4,004 |
| 175 | 7,106 | 3,827 | 6,233 | 8,694 | 2,276 | 4,315 |
| 185 | 7,479 | 4,038 | 6,233 | 8,894 | 2,276 | 4,615 |
| 195 | 7,846 | 4,261 | 6,233 | 8,973 | 2,276 | 4,902 |
| 205 | 8,210 | 4,499 | 6,233 | 8,981 | 2,276 | 5,172 |
| 215 | 8,573 | 4,756 | 6,233 | 8,981 | 2,276 | 5,424 |
| 225 | 8,939 | 5,034 | 6,233 | 8,981 | 2,276 | 5,654 |
| 235 | 9,309 | 5,337 | 6,233 | 8,981 | 2,276 | 5,860 |
| 245 | 9,688 | 5,667 | 6,233 | 8,981 | 2,276 | 6,038 |
| 255 | 10,078 | 6,028 | 6,233 | 8,981 | 2,276 | 6,185 |

**Table 10—Yield tables for the Rocky Mountain South region by forest type**

| Age class | Douglas-fir | Ponderosa pine | Fir-spruce | Lodgepole pine | Hardwood | Pinyon juniper | High-elevation softwoods |
|-----------|-------------|----------------|------------|----------------|----------|----------------|---------------------------|
| | | | *Cubic feet per acre* | | | | |
| 5 | 0 | 0 | 0 | 0 | 0 | 0 | 0 |
| 15 | 15 | 0 | 39 | 5 | 5 | 3 | 0 |
| 25 | 104 | 33 | 254 | 25 | 65 | 26 | 41 |
| 35 | 242 | 122 | 553 | 46 | 202 | 62 | 234 |
| 45 | 409 | 245 | 901 | 116 | 407 | 108 | 584 |
| 55 | 597 | 388 | 1,279 | 287 | 669 | 159 | 994 |
| 65 | 799 | 542 | 1,677 | 562 | 978 | 213 | 1,415 |
| 75 | 1,013 | 704 | 2,090 | 930 | 1,323 | 270 | 1,816 |
| 85 | 1,234 | 867 | 2,513 | 1,372 | 1,695 | 328 | 2,182 |
| 95 | 1,462 | 1,031 | 2,942 | 1,867 | 2,083 | 386 | 2,502 |
| 105 | 1,692 | 1,192 | 3,375 | 2,389 | 2,478 | 444 | 2,771 |
| 115 | 1,925 | 1,349 | 3,809 | 2,909 | 2,868 | 500 | 2,989 |
| 125 | 2,159 | 1,500 | 4,243 | 3,400 | 3,243 | 554 | 3,156 |
| 135 | 2,391 | 1,645 | 4,675 | 3,830 | 3,595 | 606 | 3,275 |
| 145 | 2,621 | 1,781 | 5,105 | 4,169 | 3,911 | 654 | 3,349 |
| 155 | 2,848 | 1,909 | 5,530 | 4,386 | 4,182 | 699 | 3,385 |
| 165 | 3,070 | 2,028 | 5,951 | 4,525 | 4,399 | 739 | 3,394 |
| 175 | 3,286 | 2,136 | 6,367 | 4,650 | 4,550 | 774 | 3,394 |
| 185 | 3,495 | 2,233 | 6,776 | 4,765 | 4,625 | 804 | 3,394 |
| 195 | 3,697 | 2,320 | 7,179 | 4,870 | 4,643 | 829 | 3,394 |
| 205 | 3,889 | 2,395 | 7,574 | 4,965 | 4,643 | 846 | 3,394 |
| 215 | 4,072 | 2,457 | 7,961 | 5,050 | 4,643 | 857 | 3,394 |
| 225 | 4,245 | 2,507 | 8,340 | 5,125 | 4,643 | 861 | 3,394 |
| 235 | 4,405 | 2,545 | 8,710 | 5,190 | 4,643 | 861 | 3,394 |
| 245 | 4,553 | 2,569 | 9,071 | 5,245 | 4,643 | 861 | 3,394 |
| 255 | 4,688 | 2,580 | 9,423 | 5,290 | 4,643 | 861 | 3,394 |

**Table 11—Yield tables for the North Central Plains States region by forest type**

| Age class | Pine | Oak pine | Oak and hickory | Lowland hardwood | Maple and beech |
|---|---|---|---|---|---|
| | | | *Cubic feet per acre* | | |
| 5 | 0 | 0 | 0 | 0 | 0 |
| 15 | 116 | 65 | 34 | 40 | 15 |
| 25 | 575 | 406 | 191 | 271 | 159 |
| 35 | 1,000 | 828 | 387 | 603 | 424 |
| 45 | 1,366 | 1,239 | 617 | 977 | 750 |
| 55 | 1,682 | 1,618 | 874 | 1,368 | 1,109 |
| 65 | 1,956 | 1,959 | 1,153 | 1,762 | 1,484 |
| 75 | 2,192 | 2,259 | 1,448 | 2,148 | 1,865 |
| 85 | 2,397 | 2,515 | 1,753 | 2,519 | 2,246 |
| 95 | 2,574 | 2,727 | 2,062 | 2,872 | 2,619 |
| 105 | 2,724 | 2,893 | 2,370 | 3,200 | 2,982 |
| 115 | 2,851 | 3,014 | 2,671 | 3,502 | 3,330 |
| 125 | 2,958 | 3,088 | 2,959 | 3,775 | 3,662 |
| 135 | 3,044 | 3,115 | 3,228 | 4,016 | 3,974 |
| 145 | 3,112 | 3,117 | 3,472 | 4,224 | 4,264 |
| 155 | 3,163 | 3,117 | 3,686 | 4,397 | 4,531 |
| 165 | 3,199 | 3,117 | 3,863 | 4,534 | 4,774 |
| 175 | 3,219 | 3,117 | 3,999 | 4,634 | 4,991 |
| 185 | 3,226 | 3,117 | 4,087 | 4,695 | 5,181 |
| 195 | 3,226 | 3,117 | 4,121 | 4,717 | 5,344 |
| 205 | 3,226 | 3,117 | 4,124 | 4,718 | 5,477 |
| 215 | 3,226 | 3,117 | 4,124 | 4,718 | 5,581 |
| 225 | 3,226 | 3,117 | 4,124 | 4,718 | 5,654 |
| 235 | 3,226 | 3,117 | 4,124 | 4,718 | 5,697 |
| 245 | 3,226 | 3,117 | 4,124 | 4,718 | 5,710 |
| 255 | 3,226 | 3,117 | 4,124 | 4,718 | 5,710 |

**Table 12—Yield tables for the North Central Lake States region by forest type**

| Age class | Jack pine | Red pine | White pine | Spruce and balsam fir | Swamp conifer | Oak and hickory | Lowland hardwood | Maple and beech | Aspen and birch |
|---|---|---|---|---|---|---|---|---|---|
| | | | | *Cubic feet per acre* | | | | | |
| 5 | 0 | 0 | 0 | 0 | 0 | 0 | 0 | 0 | 0 |
| 15 | 30 | 103 | 31 | 53 | 21 | 33 | 34 | 48 | 38 |
| 25 | 228 | 775 | 272 | 315 | 119 | 232 | 216 | 312 | 285 |
| 35 | 538 | 1,688 | 689 | 668 | 258 | 527 | 468 | 686 | 668 |
| 45 | 899 | 2,544 | 1,201 | 1,092 | 444 | 874 | 760 | 1,115 | 1,119 |
| 55 | 1,284 | 3,315 | 1,768 | 1,565 | 664 | 1,252 | 1,079 | 1,576 | 1,604 |
| 65 | 1,677 | 4,003 | 2,370 | 2,065 | 909 | 1,647 | 1,413 | 2,055 | 2,106 |
| 75 | 2,068 | 4,614 | 2,992 | 2,572 | 1,171 | 2,054 | 1,758 | 2,542 | 2,613 |
| 85 | 2,450 | 5,154 | 3,624 | 3,063 | 1,446 | 2,466 | 2,105 | 3,030 | 3,116 |
| 95 | 2,817 | 5,631 | 4,259 | 3,517 | 1,728 | 2,878 | 2,452 | 3,516 | 3,609 |
| 105 | 3,164 | 6,049 | 4,891 | 3,914 | 2,014 | 3,289 | 2,794 | 3,995 | 4,087 |
| 115 | 3,490 | 6,412 | 5,515 | 4,232 | 2,302 | 3,695 | 3,127 | 4,464 | 4,546 |
| 125 | 3,791 | 6,726 | 6,128 | 4,449 | 2,589 | 4,093 | 3,447 | 4,921 | 4,983 |
| 135 | 4,064 | 6,994 | 6,726 | 4,544 | 2,874 | 4,484 | 3,752 | 5,364 | 5,395 |
| 145 | 4,308 | 7,217 | 7,307 | 4,559 | 3,155 | 4,864 | 4,038 | 5,791 | 5,781 |
| 155 | 4,521 | 7,401 | 7,868 | 4,559 | 3,431 | 5,233 | 4,302 | 6,200 | 6,137 |
| 165 | 4,702 | 7,545 | 8,408 | 4,559 | 3,700 | 5,589 | 4,541 | 6,591 | 6,463 |
| 175 | 4,849 | 7,654 | 8,925 | 4,559 | 3,961 | 5,932 | 4,753 | 6,962 | 6,757 |
| 185 | 4,962 | 7,728 | 9,417 | 4,559 | 4,213 | 6,261 | 4,934 | 7,312 | 7,018 |
| 195 | 5,039 | 7,770 | 9,882 | 4,559 | 4,455 | 6,575 | 5,082 | 7,641 | 7,244 |
| 205 | 5,080 | 7,783 | 10,321 | 4,559 | 4,688 | 6,874 | 5,194 | 7,947 | 7,435 |
| 215 | 5,091 | 7,783 | 10,731 | 4,559 | 4,909 | 7,156 | 5,268 | 8,230 | 7,589 |
| 225 | 5,091 | 7,783 | 11,112 | 4,559 | 5,119 | 7,421 | 5,301 | 8,490 | 7,707 |
| 235 | 5,091 | 7,783 | 11,462 | 4,559 | 5,317 | 7,670 | 5,307 | 8,725 | 7,786 |
| 245 | 5,091 | 7,783 | 11,782 | 4,559 | 5,501 | 7,900 | 5,307 | 8,935 | 7,827 |
| 255 | 5,091 | 7,783 | 12,069 | 4,559 | 5,673 | 8,113 | 5,307 | 9,120 | 7,828 |

**Table 13—Yield tables for the Northeast region by forest type**

| Age class | Jack/red/ white pine | Spruce and balsam fir | Loblolly/ shortleaf/ oak/gum/ cypress | Oak pine | Oak hickory | Elm/ash/red maple | Maple/ beech/birch | Aspen/birch |
|---|---|---|---|---|---|---|---|---|
| | | | *Cubic feet per acre* | | | | | |
| 5 | 0 | 0 | 0 | 0 | 0 | 0 | 0 | 0 |
| 15 | 0 | 0 | 20 | 0 | 0 | 0 | 0 | 0 |
| 25 | 204 | 51 | 184 | 0 | 29 | 126 | 63 | 14 |
| 35 | 673 | 215 | 449 | 66 | 141 | 411 | 256 | 128 |
| 45 | 1,222 | 468 | 743 | 226 | 327 | 738 | 546 | 365 |
| 55 | 1,788 | 765 | 1,050 | 432 | 550 | 1,077 | 880 | 660 |
| 65 | 2,344 | 1,092 | 1,364 | 664 | 793 | 1,414 | 1,239 | 990 |
| 75 | 2,873 | 1,439 | 1,684 | 913 | 1,051 | 1,740 | 1,614 | 1,343 |
| 85 | 3,359 | 1,804 | 2,008 | 1,176 | 1,319 | 2,050 | 1,999 | 1,712 |
| 95 | 3,793 | 2,184 | 2,334 | 1,447 | 1,594 | 2,339 | 2,392 | 2,093 |
| 105 | 4,164 | 2,578 | 2,663 | 1,726 | 1,875 | 2,601 | 2,791 | 2,484 |
| 115 | 4,462 | 2,986 | 2,993 | 2,011 | 2,161 | 2,833 | 3,193 | 2,882 |
| 125 | 4,679 | 3,407 | 3,325 | 2,300 | 2,450 | 3,030 | 3,599 | 3,287 |
| 135 | 4,806 | 3,841 | 3,658 | 2,593 | 2,743 | 3,190 | 4,008 | 3,696 |
| 145 | 4,845 | 4,289 | 3,991 | 2,890 | 3,038 | 3,307 | 4,419 | 4,110 |
| 155 | 4,845 | 4,751 | 4,326 | 3,189 | 3,336 | 3,379 | 4,831 | 4,528 |
| 165 | 4,845 | 5,228 | 4,661 | 3,491 | 3,635 | 3,404 | 5,245 | 4,949 |
| 175 | 4,845 | 5,720 | 4,997 | 3,795 | 3,936 | 3,404 | 5,659 | 5,372 |

**Table 14—Yield tables for the Southern (South Central and Southeast) regions by forest type**

| Age class | Planted pine | Natural pine | Oak pine | Upland hardwood | Bottomland hardwood |
|---|---|---|---|---|---|
| | | *Cubic feet per acre* | | | |
| 5 | 0 | 0 | 0 | 0 | 0 |
| 10 | 331 | 273 | 195 | 167 | 140 |
| 15 | 1,167 | 525 | 397 | 303 | 284 |
| 20 | 2,067 | 863 | 628 | 483 | 467 |
| 25 | 2,782 | 1,222 | 848 | 666 | 649 |
| 30 | 3,211 | 1,554 | 1,104 | 860 | 830 |
| 35 | 3,360 | 1,875 | 1,384 | 1,091 | 1,049 |
| 40 | 3,439 | 2,177 | 1,675 | 1,348 | 1,318 |
| 45 | 3,517 | 2,462 | 1,950 | 1,630 | 1,582 |
| 50 | 3,595 | 2,736 | 2,202 | 1,901 | 1,830 |
| 55 | 3,675 | 2,978 | 2,450 | 2,164 | 2,091 |
| 60 | 3,755 | 3,200 | 2,710 | 2,414 | 2,374 |
| 65 | 3,835 | 3,407 | 2,923 | 2,652 | 2,664 |
| 70 | 3,915 | 3,614 | 3,127 | 2,880 | 2,940 |
| 75 | 3,995 | 3,782 | 3,352 | 3,082 | 3,180 |
| 80 | 4,075 | 3,960 | 3,539 | 3,278 | 3,400 |
| 85 | 4,155 | 4,138 | 3,707 | 3,465 | 3,677 |
| 90 | 4,235 | 4,280 | 3,891 | 3,632 | 3,986 |